THE 2024 TOTAL SOLAR ECLIPSE

SERIES OF ASTRONOMICAL EVENTS TO
LOOK OUT FOR IN 2024

KATE OTTIS

Copyright © [2024] [KATE OTTIS]

All rights reserved. No part of this publication may be reproduced, distributed, or transmitted in any form or by any means, including photocopying, recording, or other electronic or mechanical methods, without the prior written permission of the publisher, except in the case of brief quotations embodied in critical reviews and certain other noncommercial uses permitted by copyright law. This book is a work of fiction. Names, characters, places, and incidents either are the product of the author's imagination or are used fictitiously, and any resemblance to actual persons, living or dead, events, or locales is entirely coincidental.

Table of Contents

INTRODUCTION 5
CHAPTER 1 9
  WHAT IS AN ECLIPSE? 9
    ECLIPSES THAT HAVE OCCURED 15
CHAPTER 2 19
  Stages of a Total Solar Eclipse 19
    Partial Eclipse 19
    Shadow Bands 20
    Baily's Beads 21
    Diamond Ring 22
    Totality 23
    Brightening Reappears 24
    Diamond Ring, Baily's Beads, and Shadow Bands – Again .. 25
  The Impact of Eclipses on Earth 25
  Astronomical Events in 2024 27
CHAPTER 3 33
  Why 2024's Total Solar Eclipse Will Be So Special 33
  THE ECLIPSE PATH 35
  HOW DO YOU SAFELY WATCH AN ECLIPSE? 39
  Eye Safety During a Total Solar Eclipse 39
    Skin Safety 46
  General Questions 55
    How long will the 2024 total solar eclipse last? 55
    What does the path of totality mean? 55

How much will daylight change during a total solar eclipse?..55

How big of a temperature drop do you get during a total solar eclipse? 55

What are the stages of a total solar eclipse?...................55

Why is it not safe to look at the Sun even when only a small part of it is visible?..57

Is it true that you should not look at the Sun even during a total solar eclipse?..57

How are eyes damaged by staring at the Sun?...............58

Where can I get the right kind of solar filter to view the eclipse? 59

Is it only the bright light that is dangerous when viewing the Sun? 59

Can I photograph the eclipse with my smartphone?............60

How do modern-day scientists predict eclipses? 60

How rare are total solar eclipses? 61

How is a total solar eclipse unique? 61

Why do NASA scientists' study solar eclipses? 62

How is the Sun completely blocked in a total eclipse?..........62

EDUCATIONAL RESOURSES 63

INTRODUCTION

In the vast world of cosmic phenomena, few events capture the imagination and awe of humanity like a total solar eclipse. The year 2024 marks a significant milestone in celestial events, with a total solar eclipse set to grace the skies in a breathtaking display of nature's magnificence. "The 2024 Total Solar Eclipse" serves as a comprehensive guide to this rare and awe-inspiring event, offering readers a deeper understanding of the eclipse phenomenon and practical tips for experiencing it firsthand.

This book delves into the science behind solar eclipses, explaining the alignment of celestial bodies that leads to this extraordinary event. From the movement of the Earth, Moon, and Sun to the precise calculations that predict the path of totality, readers will gain insights into the cosmic mechanics that create such a mesmerizing spectacle.

In addition to revealing the science and history of solar eclipses, this book is a practical guide for enthusiasts eager to witness the 2024 event. It provides detailed information on best viewing locations, safety precautions, and equipment needed to fully appreciate the eclipse's beauty without risking eye damage or missing the rare spectacle.

As we anticipate The 2024 Total Solar Eclipse here are some series of Astronomical Events to Look Out for in 2024:

1. The Great North American Eclipse: The total solar eclipse on April 8, 2024, will be visible across North America, creating a path of totality that stretches from Mexico to Canada. This event is a must-see for sky watchers in the region.

2. Mars Near Earth Encounter: In September 2024, Mars will make a close approach to Earth, offering astronomers a prime opportunity for observing the Red Planet in detail.

3. Jupiter and Saturn Conjunction: Towards the end of 2024, Jupiter and Saturn will appear close together in the sky, forming a stunning conjunction that will be visible to the naked eye.

4. Meteor Showers: Throughout the year, several meteor showers, such as the Perseids in August and the Geminids in December, will grace the night skies, providing dazzling displays for avid stargazers.

5. Lunar Eclipses: Keep an eye out for lunar eclipses in 2024, which occur when the Earth passes between the Sun and the Moon, casting a shadow that creates a dramatic lunar spectacle.

These astronomical events, combined with the highlight of the total solar eclipse, make 2024 a year of celestial wonders and opportunities for exploration and discovery in the night sky.

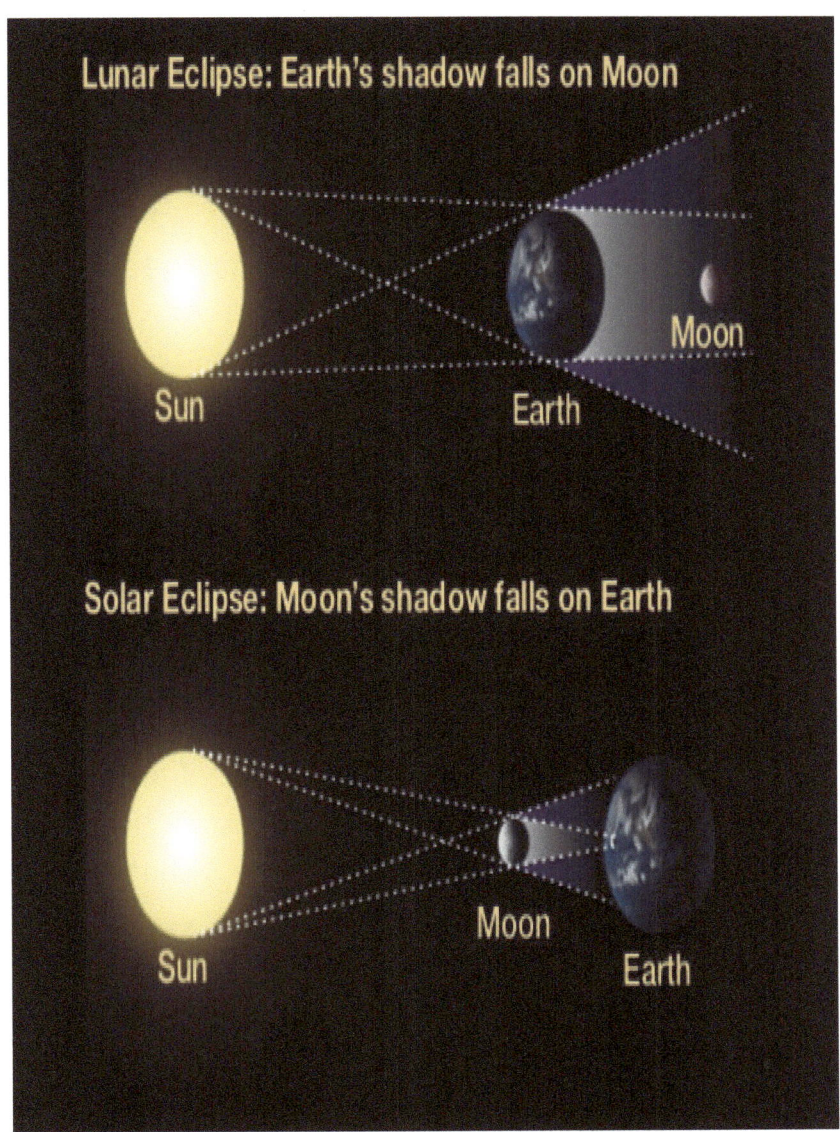

CHAPTER 1

WHAT IS AN ECLIPSE?

An eclipse is an astronomical event that occurs when one celestial body moves into the shadow of another celestial body, causing a partial or total obstruction of the first body's light.

There are two main types:

Solar Eclipse:

A solar eclipse occurs when the Moon passes directly between the Earth and the Sun, casting its shadow on the Earth's surface. This alignment of the three celestial bodies happens during a new moon phase. There are three types of solar eclipses:

1. Total Solar Eclipse: In a total solar eclipse, the Moon completely covers the Sun, momentarily blocking out its light. This creates a dark shadow on Earth known as the **umbra**, where observers experience totality – a breathtaking phenomenon where the Sun's outer atmosphere, the corona, becomes visible. Total solar eclipses are visible only along a narrow path on Earth's surface

2. Partial Solar Eclipse: During a partial solar eclipse, the Moon partially covers the Sun, resulting in a

fraction of its light being blocked. Observers outside the path of totality witness a partial eclipse, where a portion of the Sun remains visible. This occurs when the alignment between the Sun, Moon, and Earth is not perfectly straight.

3. Annular Solar Eclipse: An annular solar eclipse happens when the Moon is farther away from Earth in its elliptical orbit, appearing smaller in the sky. As a result, it doesn't fully cover the Sun, leaving a ring of sunlight visible around the edges of the Moon. Annular eclipses occur when the Moon is near its apogee, the farthest point from Earth.

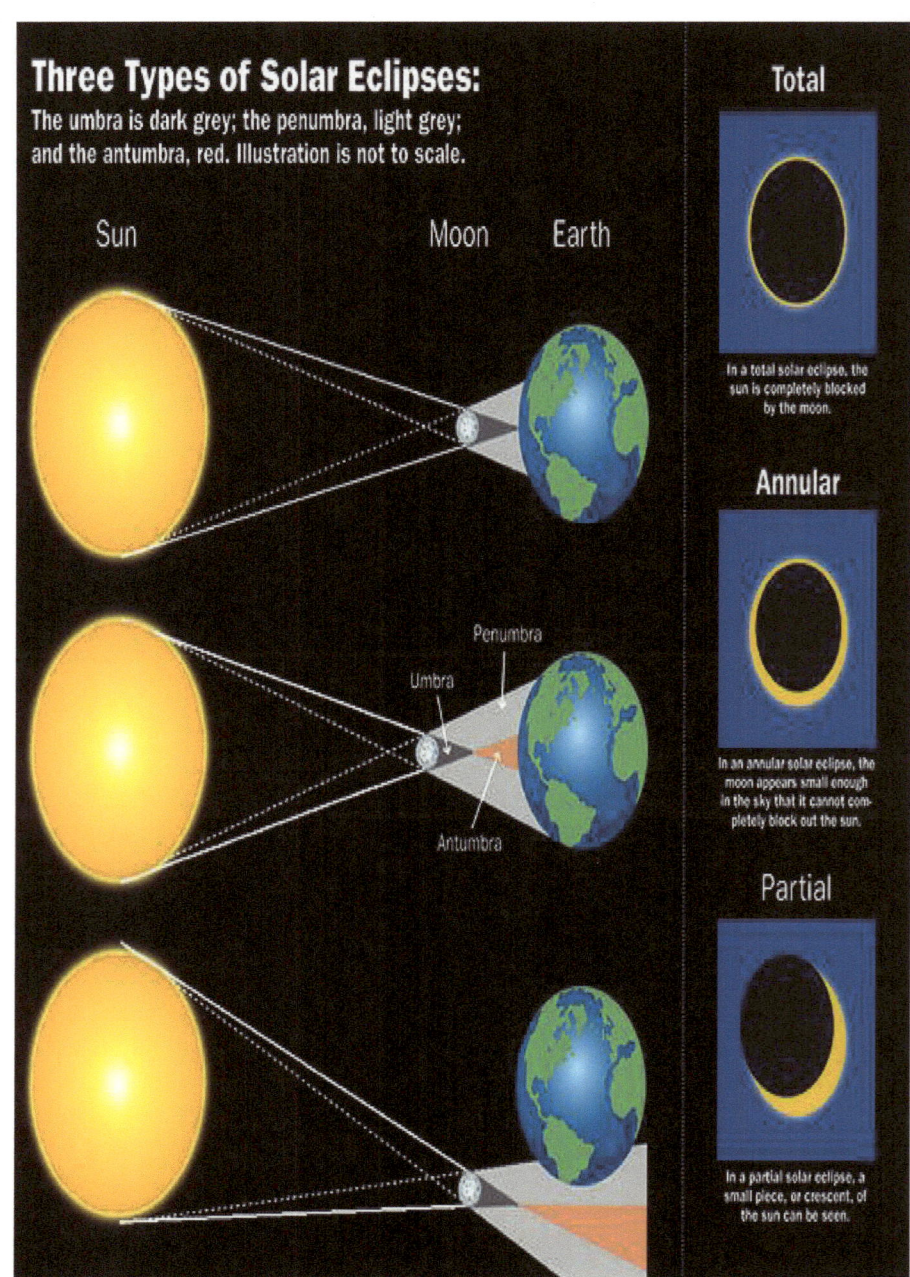

Lunar Eclipse:

A lunar eclipse occurs when the Earth passes between the Sun and the Moon, causing the Earth's shadow to fall on the lunar surface. This alignment typically happens during a full moon phase. There are three types of lunar eclipses:

1. Total Lunar Eclipse: During a total lunar eclipse, the entire Moon passes through the Earth's umbral shadow, causing it to appear red or coppery in color. This reddish hue is due to the scattering of sunlight by Earth's atmosphere, with longer wavelengths (red) being refracted more than shorter wavelengths (blue). This phenomenon is often called a "blood moon."

2. Partial Lunar Eclipse: In a partial lunar eclipse, only a part of the Moon enters the Earth's umbral shadow, resulting in a portion of the Moon being darkened. The rest of the lunar surface remains unaffected.

3. Penumbral Lunar Eclipse :A penumbral lunar eclipse occurs when the Moon passes through the Earth's penumbral shadow, the outer part of the shadow where the Sun is only partially blocked. This results in a subtle darkening of the lunar surface that may be difficult to discern without careful observation.

HOW DO SOLAR ECLIPSES DIFFER FROM LUNAR ECLIPSES?

Lunar eclipses occur when Earth is positioned between the moon and the sun and our planet's shadow is cast upon the lunar surface. This leaves the moon looking dim from Earth, sometimes with a reddish color. Lunar eclipses are visible from half of Earth, a much wider area than solar eclipses.

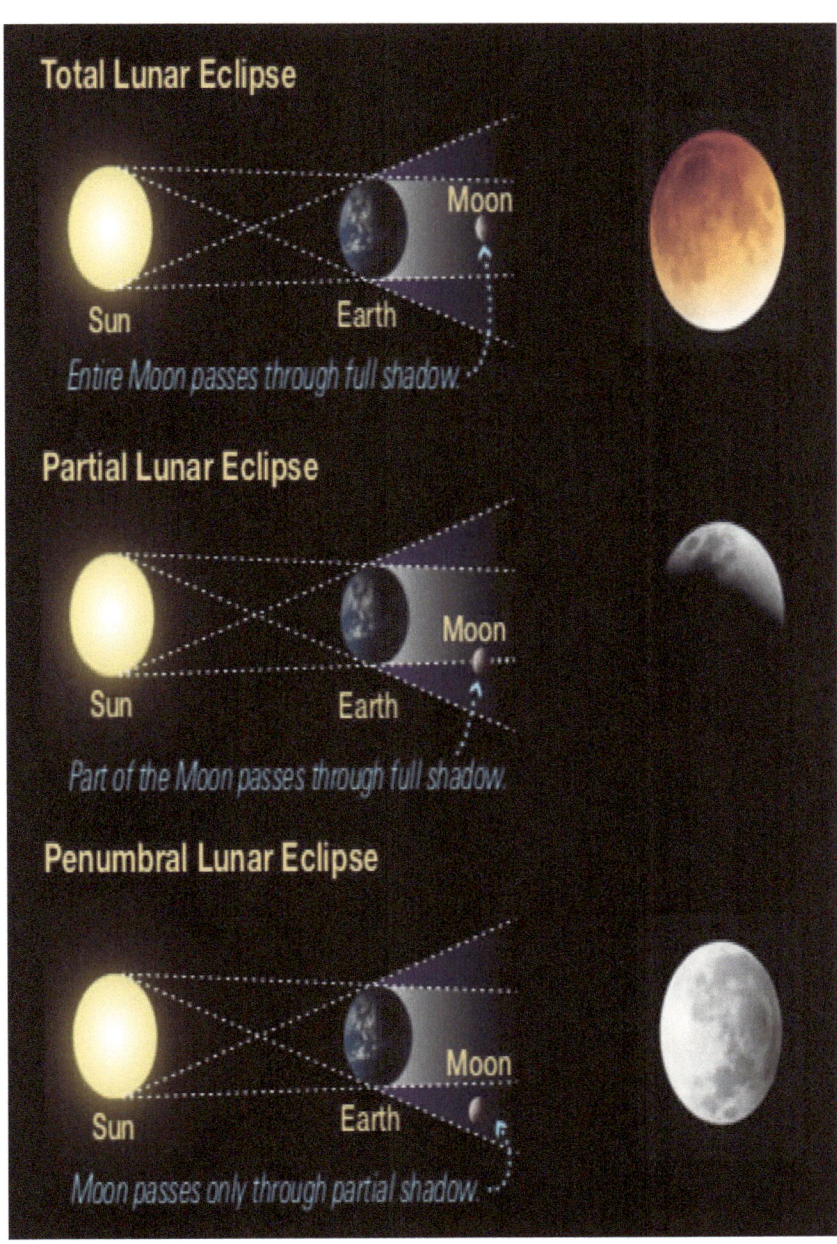

ECLIPSES THAT HAVE OCCURED

Eclipses are relatively rare events and are often accompanied by unique visual phenomena and scientific interest, Eclipses provide not only spectacular celestial events but also valuable opportunities for scientific study. They have played significant roles throughout history in advancing our understanding of the cosmos and continue to captivate observers worldwide with their beauty and mystery.

Solar Eclipses that have occurred

May 28, 585 BC: The eclipse during the Battle of Halys between the Medes and the Lydians in ancient Anatolia (modern-day Turkey) is often cited as one of the earliest recorded instances of humans predicting an eclipse. According to Herodotus, the Greek philosopher Thales of Miletus accurately predicted the eclipse, which interrupted the battle and led to a truce between the warring parties.

May 10, 610 AD: A total solar eclipse occurred over the Arabian Peninsula, during the early years of Islam. This eclipse is historically significant as it coincided with the death of Muhammad's son Ibrahim, leading to various interpretations and religious reflections within the Islamic community.

May 3, 1715: Known as the "Eclipse of Louis XIV," this total solar eclipse was visible across Europe, with the path of totality crossing through France. King Louis XIV of France reportedly saw the eclipse from his palace at Versailles, which fueled discussions about the nature of celestial phenomena and scientific inquiry during the Enlightenment period.

July 8, 1842: A total solar eclipse traveled across Europe and Asia, providing a rare opportunity for astronomers to study the Sun's corona. This eclipse was particularly significant as it occurred during the infancy of astrophotography, allowing scientists to capture images of the solar corona for the first time.

May 29, 1919: The solar eclipse observed in Sobral, Brazil, and Príncipe Island in West Africa became famous for its role in validating Albert Einstein's theory of general relativity. British astronomer Sir Arthur Eddington led an expedition to measure the apparent shift of star positions near the Sun during the eclipse, providing experimental evidence supporting Einstein's predictions.

June 30, 1954: A total solar eclipse occurred over Northern Europe, with the path of totality passing through Sweden, Norway, and Finland. This eclipse garnered significant attention from scientists and the public, as it coincided with the International Geophysical Year, a global initiative aimed at promoting scientific cooperation and exploration.

July 22, 2009: A total solar eclipse traveled across India, Nepal, Bhutan, Bangladesh, Myanmar, China, and the Pacific Ocean. Millions of people witnessed the event, which prompted cultural celebrations, scientific research, and efforts to raise awareness about safe viewing practices.

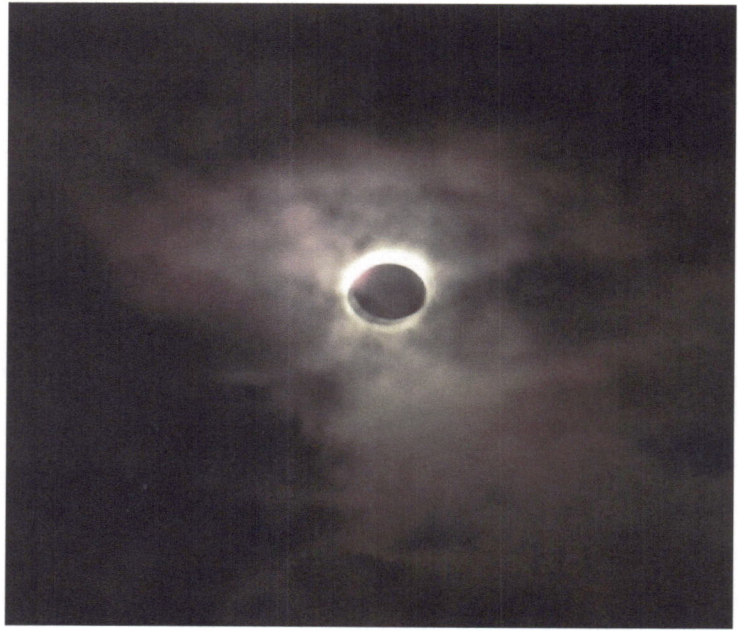

December 26, 2019: The "Ring of Fire" annular solar eclipse occurred, visible from Saudi Arabia, India, Sri Lanka, Indonesia, the Philippines, and Guam. This eclipse attracted widespread attention due to its unique annular phase, where the Moon does not fully cover the Sun, resulting in a ring-like appearance.

These eclipses represent a diverse array of historical, cultural, and scientific contexts, each contributing to humanity's understanding of astronomy.

CHAPTER 2

Stages of a Total Solar Eclipse

There are several distinct stages of a total solar eclipse that observers can watch for. You must not remove your eclipse glasses until the Moon has completely covered the Sun, the portion of the eclipse known as "totality."

Partial Eclipse

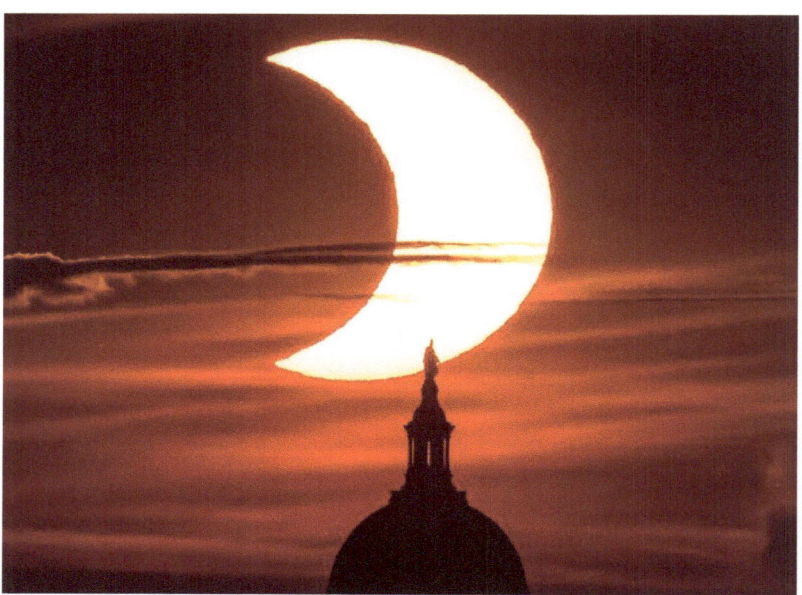

As the Moon passes between the Sun and Earth, at first it does not completely cover the Sun. The Sun appears to have a crescent shape. For most locations, the partial eclipse phase will last between 70 and 80 minutes. Your eclipse glasses must be worn when viewing the Sun during the partial eclipse phase. The moment when the Moon first "touches" the Sun is also called the first contact.

Shadow Bands
Shadow bands are rapidly moving, long, dark bands separated by white spaces that can be seen on the sides of buildings or the ground just before and after totality, though they can be very faint and difficult to photograph. Earth's upper atmosphere contains turbulent cells of air that distort the sharp-edged light from the solar surface, the same way it distorts starlight and causes stars to twinkle.

Baily's Beads

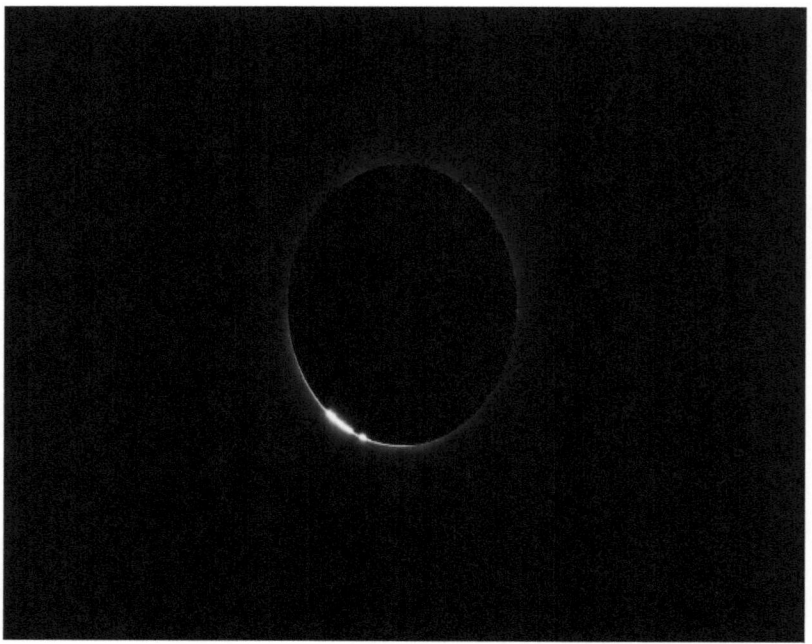

As the Moon continues to move across the Sun, several points of light shine around the Moon's edges. Known as Baily's Beads, these are light rays from the Sun streaming through the valleys along the Moon's horizon. Baily's Beads are very short-lived, and may not last long enough to be noticeable to all observers of the total solar eclipse.

Diamond Ring

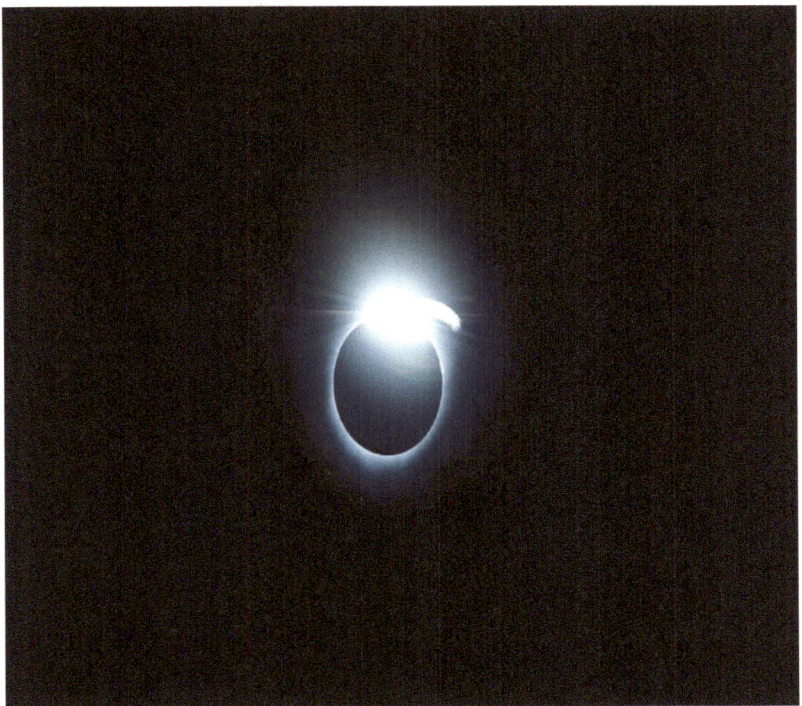

Baily's Beads will begin to disappear until eventually only a single bright spot will remain along the edge of the Moon's shadow. This bright spot resembles the diamond in a giant diamond ring formed by the rest of the Sun's atmosphere. Totality is almost here.

Totality

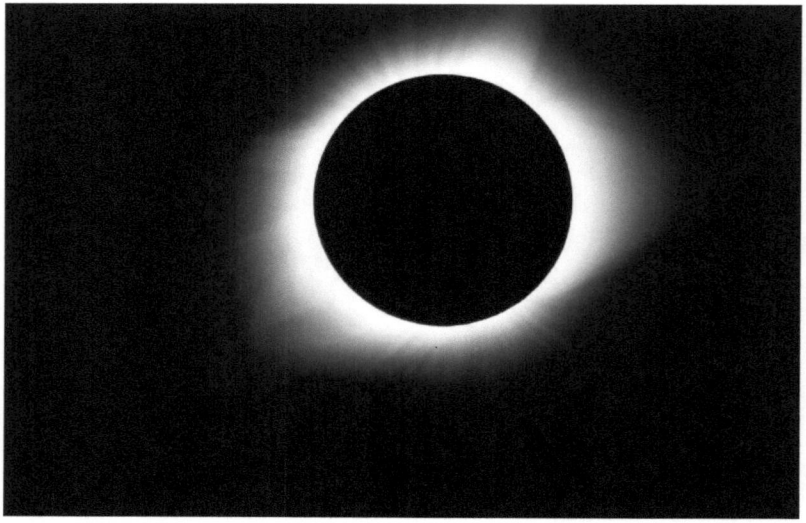

Once the diamond ring disappears and there is no longer any direct sunlight, you may remove your eclipse glasses and look at the total eclipse safely with the naked eye. This moment is also called second contact. During totality, viewers may be able to see the chromosphere (a region of the solar atmosphere, appearing as the thin circle of pink around the Moon) and the corona (the outer solar atmosphere, appearing as streams of white light). Be vigilant to protect your eyes and put your eclipse glasses back on before totality ends. Totality may last only a minute or two in some locations.

During totality, take a few seconds to observe the world around you. You may be able to see a 360-degree sunset. You may also be able to see some particularly bright stars or planets in the darkened sky. The air temperature will drop and often an eerie silence will settle around you. It is also worth stealing a peek at the people around you – many people have a deep emotional response when the Sun goes into totality.

Brightening Reappears

As the Moon continues to move across the face of the Sun, you will begin to see brightening on the opposite side from where the diamond ring shone at the beginning. This is the lower atmosphere of the Sun, beginning to peek out from behind the Moon and it is your signal to stop looking directly at the eclipse. Make sure your eclipse glasses are back on – or you are otherwise watching the eclipse through a safe, indirect method – before the first flash of sunlight appears around the edges of the Moon. This moment is also called third contact.

Diamond Ring, Baily's Beads, and Shadow Bands – Again

Once your eyes are protected again, you may continue to watch the final stages of the eclipse as the end process mirrors the beginning: You will again see the diamond ring, Baily's Beads, and shadow bands before the entire Sun is visible. Fourth contact is the moment that none of the Sun is covered by the Moon's shadow. This is when the eclipse is completely over, but most likely you will have already packed up your things and began planning your next eclipse adventure

The Impact of Eclipses on Earth

Solar and lunar eclipses have intrigued and influenced humans throughout history, not only because of their spectacular visual impact but also due to their effects on various aspects of life on Earth. Here are some ways eclipses impact our planet:

1. Climate and Weather Patterns:

During a solar eclipse, the sudden decrease in sunlight can lead to a temporary drop in temperature in the eclipse's path. This phenomenon, known as the "eclipse cooling effect," can be observed as a localized cooling of the Earth's surface.

Scientists study these temperature changes to better understand the relationship between solar radiation and climate patterns. Eclipses provide valuable data for climate modeling and research into Earth's energy balance.

2. Animal Behavior:

Animals often exhibit unusual behaviors during eclipses. Birds may stop singing, nocturnal animals may become active, and domesticated animals may show signs of confusion or agitation.

Researchers study these behavioral changes to learn more about how animals perceive and respond to changes in light and environmental cues. Eclipses offer a unique opportunity to observe these natural reactions in controlled settings.

3. Scientific Discoveries:

Eclipses have historically played a crucial role in advancing scientific knowledge. For example, during a total solar eclipse in 1919, astronomers observed the bending of starlight around the Sun, confirming Einstein's theory of general relativity.

Modern eclipses continue to inspire scientific research and discoveries. Astronomers use eclipses to study the Sun's corona, solar flares, and magnetic fields, leading to insights into solar physics and space weather.

4. Public Interest and Education:

Eclipses capture public attention and interest in astronomy and science. They provide opportunities for outreach and education, encouraging people of all ages to learn about celestial phenomena and the importance of scientific inquiry.

Events like total solar eclipses draw large crowds of spectators, creating opportunities for public engagement, citizen science projects, and collaborative research efforts.

Astronomical Events in 2024

Let's look into the notable astronomical events happening in 2024, including lunar eclipses, planetary alignments, meteor showers, and rare celestial occurrences:

Lunar Eclipses:

May 15, 2024: This total lunar eclipse will be visible from regions spanning North America, South

America, Europe, Africa, and Asia. During totality, the moon takes on a reddish or coppery hue, often referred to as a "blood moon" due to the scattering of sunlight by Earth's atmosphere.

November 7, 2024: Another total lunar eclipse occurs, visible from parts of North America, South America, Asia, Australia, and the Pacific region. Lunar eclipses provide captivating opportunities to observe the Earth's shadow gradually engulfing and then revealing the moon in striking shades of red and orange.

Solar Eclipses:

October 2, 2024: A partial solar eclipse takes place, observable from South America, including Brazil and Argentina. During a partial solar eclipse, a portion of the sun is obscured by the moon, creating a crescent-shaped sun when viewed from Earth.

Aside from the partial eclipse, the highlight of 2024 is the April 8 total solar eclipse, as discussed earlier, which traverses North America and parts of Mexico and Canada, offering a mesmerizing spectacle for skywatchers.

Planetary Alignments and Conjunctions:

Mars Opposition (August 16, 2024): Mars reaches opposition, aligning directly opposite the sun from Earth's perspective. This alignment places Mars at its closest approach to Earth, making it appear larger and brighter in the night sky. Observers can enjoy detailed views of Mars through telescopes during this period.

Jupiter Conjunctions:

May 11, 2024: Jupiter and Venus come into conjunction, forming a visually striking pairing in the evening sky. This conjunction creates a beautiful celestial sight, with the bright planets appearing close together.

October 23, 2024: Jupiter and Mercury align in conjunction, offering another intriguing planetary conjunction to observe. Mercury, being closer to the sun, presents a unique challenge for observation but can be spotted near Jupiter during this event.

Meteor Showers:

Lyrids Meteor Shower (Peak: April 22-23): The Lyrids meteor shower, originating from the debris left by Comet C/1861 G1 Thatcher, produces bright meteors that streak across the sky. Observers can expect around 10 to 20 meteors per hour during the peak, making it a modest yet enjoyable shower to watch.

Perseids Meteor Shower (Peak: August 12-13): The Perseids, associated with Comet Swift-Tuttle, are renowned for their fast and bright meteors. During the peak, observers can witness up to 100 meteors per hour under optimal viewing conditions, making it a favorite among meteor enthusiasts.

Significant Events:

Transit of Mercury (May 7, 2024): Mercury, the innermost planet, transits across the face of the sun as observed from Earth. This rare event occurs only about 13 times per century and requires proper solar viewing equipment to observe safely.

Asteroid Occultations: Throughout the year, various asteroids will pass in front of stars, causing brief occultations where the star's light is momentarily blocked. These events are of interest to astronomers studying asteroids' sizes, shapes, and orbital characteristics.

These astronomical events in 2024 offer a diverse range of celestial phenomena for observation and study, providing ample opportunities for both amateur and professional astronomers to engage with the wonders of the cosmos.

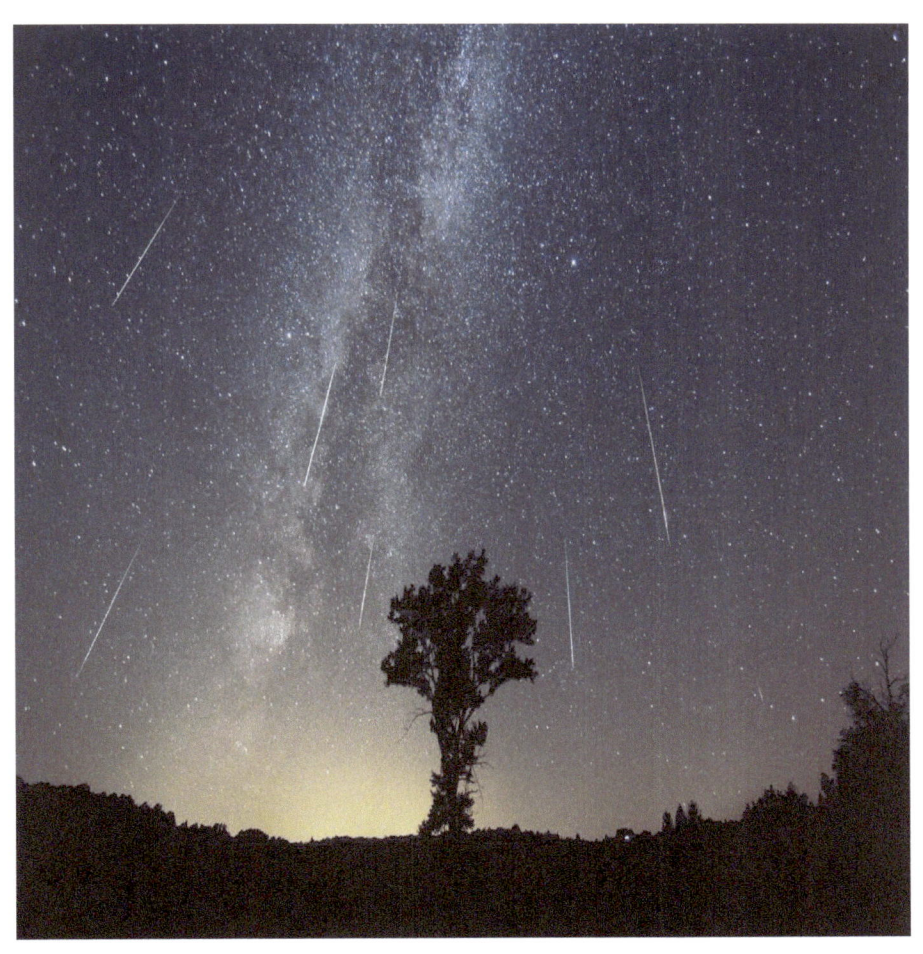

CHAPTER 3

Why 2024's Total Solar Eclipse Will Be So Special

The last time North Americans caught a total solar eclipse, the sun was in a lull of activity. This year's eclipse will be very different

A total solar eclipse that will occur this April should be spectacular in many ways, even for those who were lucky enough to catch the sun's show in 2017.

With total solar eclipses occurring only every 18 months or so and many visible only over oceans or equally inaccessible areas, any such eclipse over a densely populated region is a cause for celebration. But 2024's total solar eclipse over North America will happen when the sun is near the peak of its activity cycle. That's in stark contrast to the last great American eclipse , which occurred in august 2017, when the sun's activity was approaching a minimum.

At the magic moment of totality in 2017, when the moon was aligned precisely over the disk of the sun's visible surface, it was briefly safe to look at the convergence with bare eyes—and to catch the stunning sight of our home star's atmosphere, or corona, sketching a shallow smear of white around the moon's blackness, marked by a few shining spikes.

This April a similar total solar eclipse will grace a different swath of North America—including Mexico, Texas, Arkansas, Indiana, Ohio, upstate New York, Maine, and more. But the elusive view of the sun's corona won't look the same because this eclipse comes near the opposite end of our star's 11-year activity.

THE ECLIPSE PATH

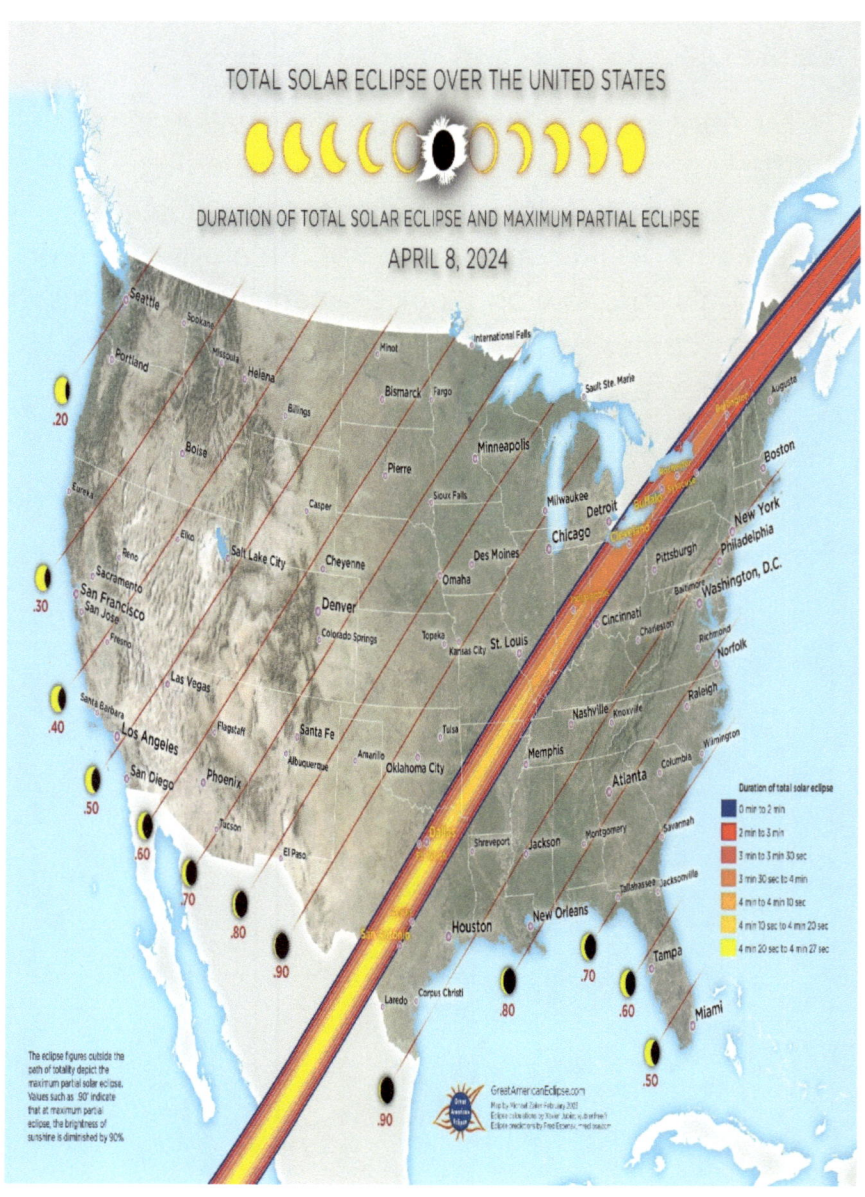

The pathway of the total solar eclipse on April 8, 2024, traverses a significant portion of North America, offering diverse landscapes and viewing experiences along its trajectory. Here's a closer look at the pathway:

1. **Starting Point:** The eclipse's path begins in the Pacific Ocean south of the Mexican state of Nayarit. It then makes landfall on the western coast of Mexico, passing over cities such as Mazatlán and Durango.

2. **Mexico:** As the eclipse progresses northeastward, it crosses central Mexico, encompassing regions like Torreón, Saltillo, and Monterrey. Observers in these areas will witness varying durations of totality based on their specific locations within the path.

3. **United States - Southern States:** Moving into the United States, the eclipse enters Texas, where cities like Del Rio, San Antonio, and Austin fall within the path of totality. Texas offers a wide range of viewing opportunities, from urban areas to more remote locations with clear skies.

4. **United States - Central States:** Continuing its journey, the eclipse crosses into states like Oklahoma, Kansas, and Missouri. Cities such as Oklahoma City, Tulsa, Wichita, Kansas City, and St.

Louis are within the path, providing accessible viewing options for a large population.

5. **United States - Midwest and Great Lakes Region:** The eclipse path extends into parts of Illinois, Indiana, Ohio, and Michigan. Notable cities like Indianapolis, Fort Wayne, Toledo, Cleveland, and Detroit will experience the total eclipse, attracting many enthusiasts and researchers.

6. **Canada:** The path then crosses into Canada, passing over the province of Ontario. Canadian cities within the path include Windsor, London, Hamilton, Toronto, and Ottawa, offering an international perspective on this celestial event.

Duration and Visibility: The duration of totality varies along the path, with the maximum duration exceeding 4 minutes in some locations. Factors such as elevation, weather conditions, and local terrain can influence the visibility and clarity of the eclipse.

Overall, the pathway of the April 8, 2024, total solar eclipse showcases the diversity of landscapes, communities, and experiences across North America, uniting people in a shared fascination with the wonders of the universe. On April 8, 2024, the moons shadow will cast on Sinaloa, Mexico and run up to Labrador, Canada crossing the continent in

Location	Partial Begins	Totality Begins	Maximum	Totality Ends	Partial Ends
Dallas, Texas	12:23 p.m. CDT	1:40 p.m. CDT	1:42 p.m. CDT	1:44 p.m. CDT	3:02 p.m. CDT
Idabel, Oklahoma	12:28 p.m. CDT	1:45 p.m. CDT	1:47 p.m. CDT	1:49 p.m. CDT	3:06 p.m. CDT
Little Rock, Arkansas	12:33 p.m. CDT	1:51 p.m. CDT	1:52 p.m. CDT	1:54 p.m. CDT	3:11 p.m. CDT
Poplar Bluff, Missouri	12:39 p.m. CDT	1:56 p.m. CDT	1:56 p.m. CDT	2:00 p.m. CDT	3:15 p.m. CDT
Paducah, Kentucky	12:42 p.m. CDT	2:00 p.m. CDT	2:01 p.m. CDT	2:02 p.m. CDT	3:18 p.m. CDT
Carbondale, Illinois	12:42 p.m. CDT	1:59 p.m. CDT	2:01 p.m. CDT	2:03 p.m. CDT	3:18 p.m. CDT
Evansville, Indiana	12:45 p.m. CDT	2:02 p.m. CDT	2:04 p.m. CDT	2:05 p.m. CDT	3:20 p.m. CDT
Cleveland, Ohio	1:59 p.m. EDT	3:13 p.m. EDT	3:15 p.m. EDT	3:17 p.m. EDT	4:29 p.m. EDT
Erie, Pennsylvania	2:02 p.m. EDT	3:16 p.m. EDT	3:18 p.m. EDT	3:20 p.m. EDT	4:30 p.m. EDT
Buffalo, New York	2:04 p.m. EDT	3:18 p.m. EDT	3:20 p.m. EDT	3:22 p.m. EDT	4:32 p.m. EDT
Burlington, Vermont	2:14 p.m. EDT	3:26 p.m. EDT	3:27 p.m. EDT	3:29 p.m. EDT	4:37 p.m. EDT
Lancaster, New Hampshire	2:16 p.m. EDT	3:27 p.m. EDT	3:29 p.m. EDT	3:30 p.m. EDT	4:38 p.m. EDT
Caribou, Maine	2:22 p.m. EDT	3:32 p.m. EDT	3:33 p.m. EDT	3:34 p.m. EDT	4:40 p.m. EDT

This table provides the time that totality begins in some U.S. cities in the path of totality. These areas will also experience a partial eclipse before and after these

HOW DO YOU SAFELY WATCH AN ECLIPSE?

Experts warn that it is unsafe to look directly at the bright sun without using specialized eye protection designed for solar viewing. Viewing an eclipse through a camera lens, binoculars or telescope without making use of a special-purpose solar filter can cause severe eye injury, according to these experts.

They advise using safe solar viewing glasses or a safe handheld solar viewer, noting that regular sunglasses are not safe for viewing the sun. The only moment it is considered safe for people to remove eye protection during a total solar eclipse is the brief time when the moon completely blocks the

Eye Safety During a Total Solar Eclipse

Except during the brief total phase of a total solar eclipse, when the Moon completely blocks the Sun's bright face, it is not safe to look directly at the Sun without specialized eye protection for solar viewing. Viewing any part of the bright Sun through a camera lens, binoculars, or a telescope without a special-purpose solar filter secured over the front of the optics will instantly cause severe eye injury.

\

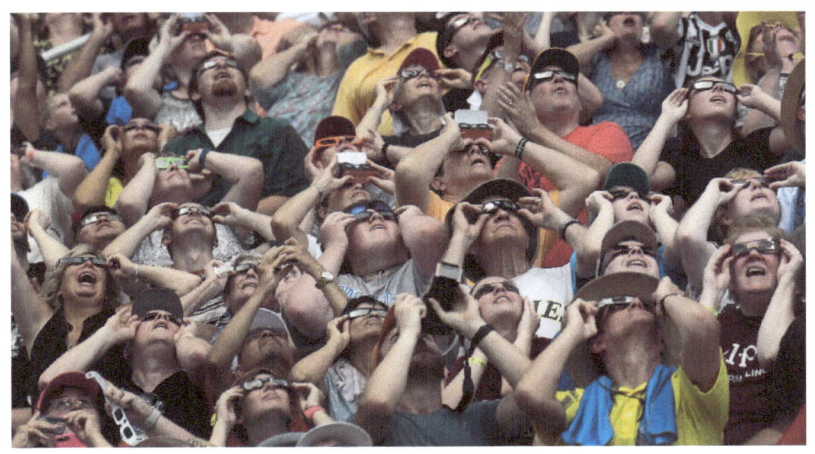

When watching the partial phases of the solar eclipse directly with your eyes, which happens before and after totality, you must look through safe solar viewing glasses ("eclipse glasses") or a safe handheld solar viewer at all times. Eclipse glasses are NOT regular sunglasses; regular sunglasses, no matter how dark, are not safe for viewing the Sun. Safe solar viewers are thousands of times darker and ought to comply with the (ISO 12312-2) international standard. NASA does not approve any particular brand of solar viewers. Always inspect your eclipse glasses or handheld viewer before use; if torn, scratched, or otherwise damaged, discard the device. Always supervise children using solar viewers.

Do NOT look at the Sun through a camera lens, telescope, binoculars, or any other optical device while wearing eclipse glasses or using a handheld solar viewer — the concentrated solar rays will burn through the filter and cause serious eye injury.

If you don't have eclipse glasses or a handheld solar viewer, you can use an **indirect viewing method**, which does not involve looking directly at the Sun. One way is to use **a pinhole projector**, which has a small opening (for example, a hole punched in an index card) and projects an image of the Sun onto a nearby surface. With the Sun at your back, you can then safely view the projected image. Do NOT look at the Sun through the pinhole!

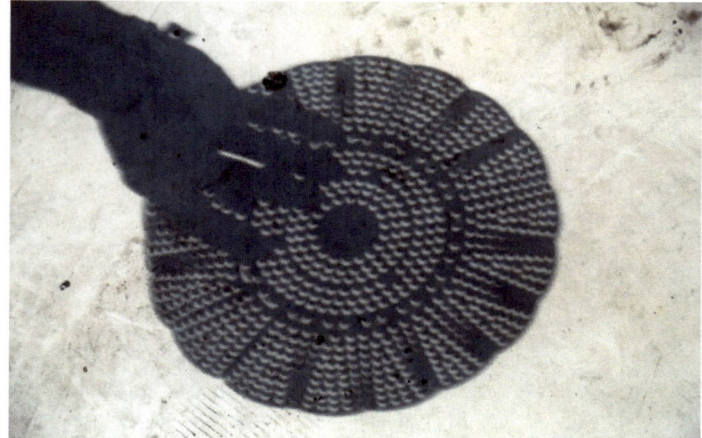

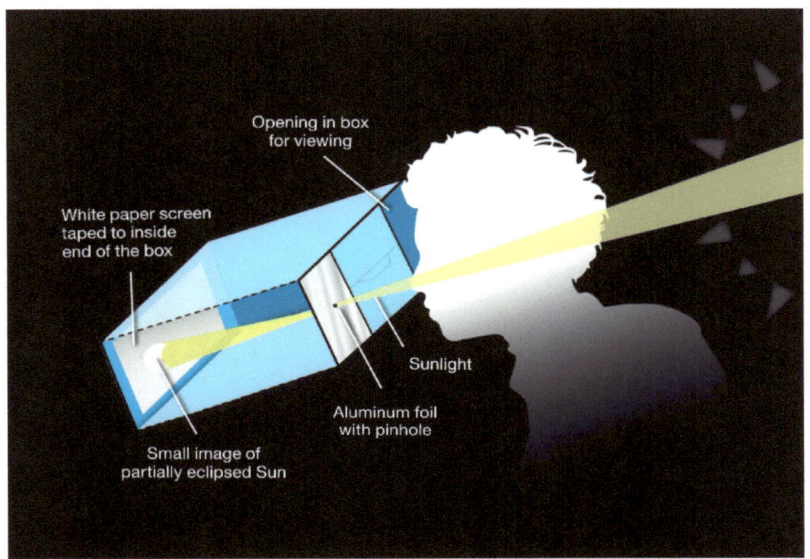

You can make your own eclipse projector using a cardboard box, a white sheet of paper, tape, scissors, and aluminum foil. With the Sun behind you, sunlight will stream through a pinhole punched into aluminum foil taped over a hole in one side of the box. During the partial phases of a solar eclipse, this will project a crescent Sun onto a white sheet of paper taped to the inside of the box. Look into the box through another hole cut into the box to see the projected image.

Do NOT use eclipse glasses or handheld viewers with cameras, binoculars, or telescopes. Those require different types of solar filters. When viewing the partial phases of the eclipse through cameras, binoculars, or telescopes equipped with proper solar filters, you do not need to wear eclipse glasses. (The solar filters do the same job as the eclipse glasses to protect your eyes.)

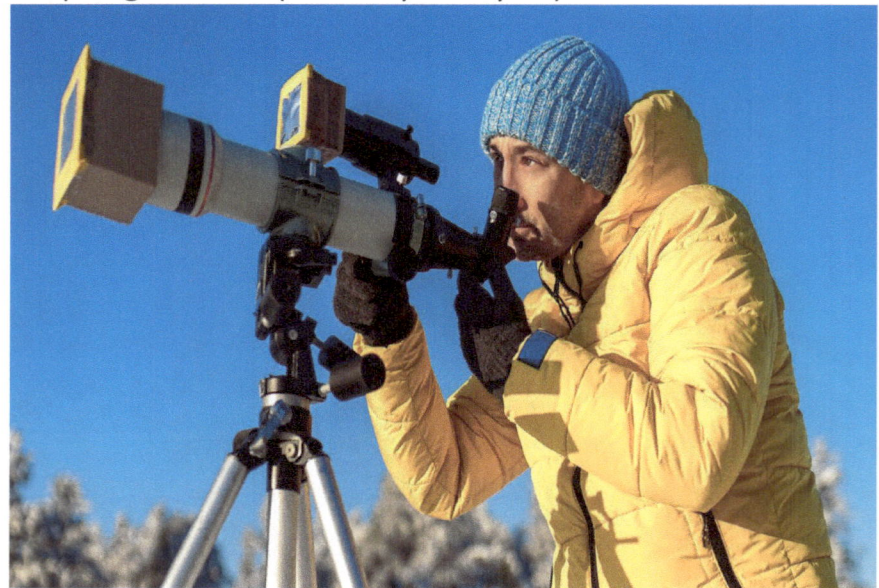

A man looks at the Sun through binoculars that have been fitted with solar filters.

Seek expert advice from an astronomer before using a solar filter with a camera, telescope, binoculars, or any other optical device. Note that solar filters must be attached to the front of any telescope, binoculars, camera lens, or other optics.

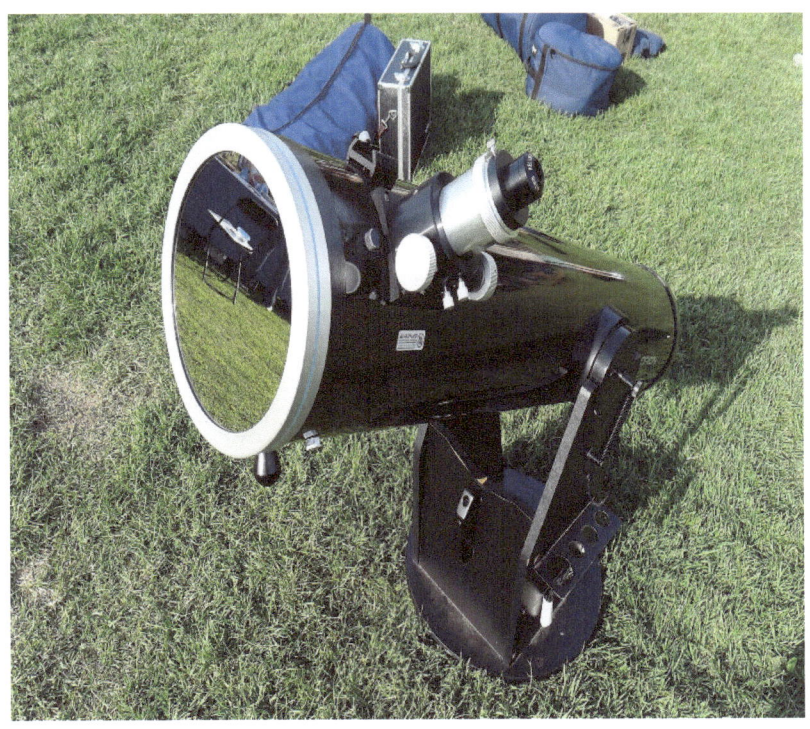

A solar filter is attached to the Sun-facing end of a telescope.

Here are some important safety guidelines to follow during a total solar eclipse.

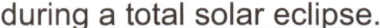

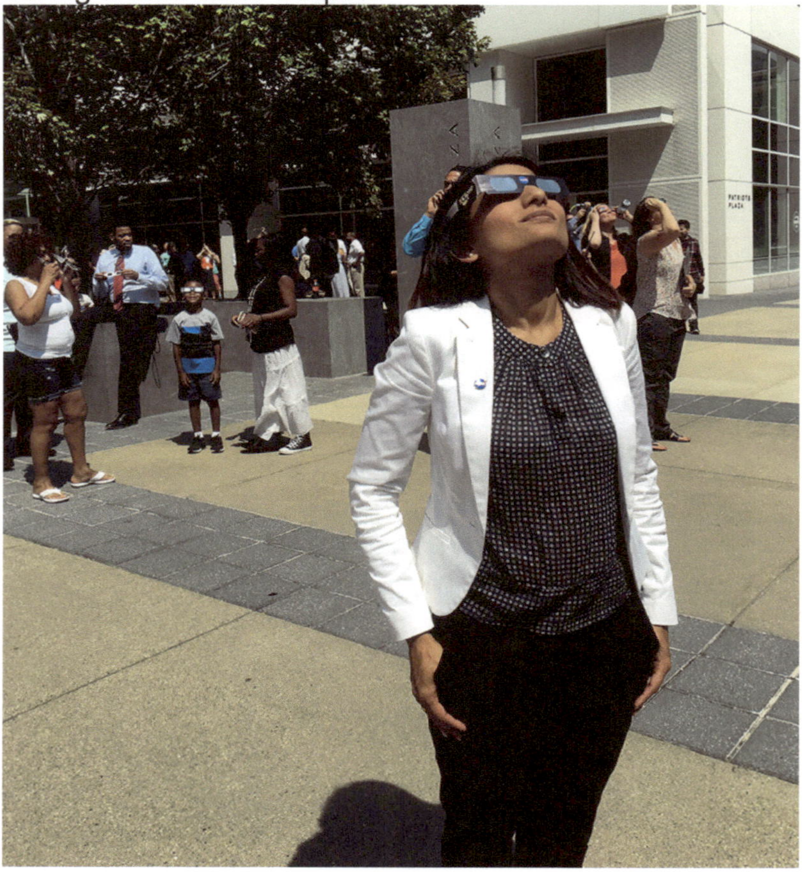

View the Sun through eclipse glasses or a handheld solar viewer during the partial eclipse phases before and after totality.

You can view the eclipse directly without proper eye protection only when the Moon completely obscures the Sun's bright face – during the brief and

46

spectacular period known as totality. (You'll know it's safe when you can no longer see any part of the Sun through eclipse glasses or a solar viewer.)

As soon as you see even a little bit of the bright Sun reappear after totality, immediately put your eclipse glasses back on or use a handheld solar viewer to look at the Sun.

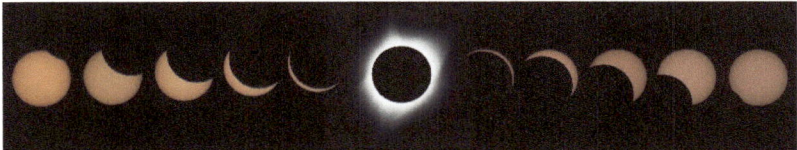

This composite image of eleven pictures shows the progression of a total solar eclipse over Madras, Oregon, on Aug. 21, 2017.

Skin Safety

Even during a partial or annular eclipse, or during the partial phases of a total eclipse, the Sun will be very bright. If you are watching an entire eclipse, you may be in direct sunlight for hours. Remember to wear sunscreen, a hat, and protective clothing to prevent skin damage

What to consider when choosing eclipse viewing equipment

Choosing the right equipment for viewing a solar eclipse is about more than just finding something to darken the bright Sun. The right gear should offer a balance between safety, optical quality, and ease of use. Here are some key factors to keep in mind:

- **Safety certification**: Look for ISO 12312-2 certification in eclipse glasses and solar viewers to ensure they meet safety standards.
- **Optical quality**: High-quality lenses and filters provide clearer and more detailed views of the eclipse.
- **Compatibility**: Ensure that telescope and camera filters are compatible with your existing equipment.
- **Comfort and portability**: Consider the comfort of wearables like glasses, as well as the portability of telescopes or binoculars.
- **Value-added features**: Extras like magnification capabilities and included accessories can enhance your viewing experience even more.

Here are some tips for photographing or filming the eclipse and other astronomical phenomena:

1. Use Proper Equipment: Invest in a good camera with manual settings, a sturdy tripod, and a telephoto lens (300mm or longer) for close-up shots of celestial events. For filming, consider a camera with high-resolution capabilities and image stabilization features.

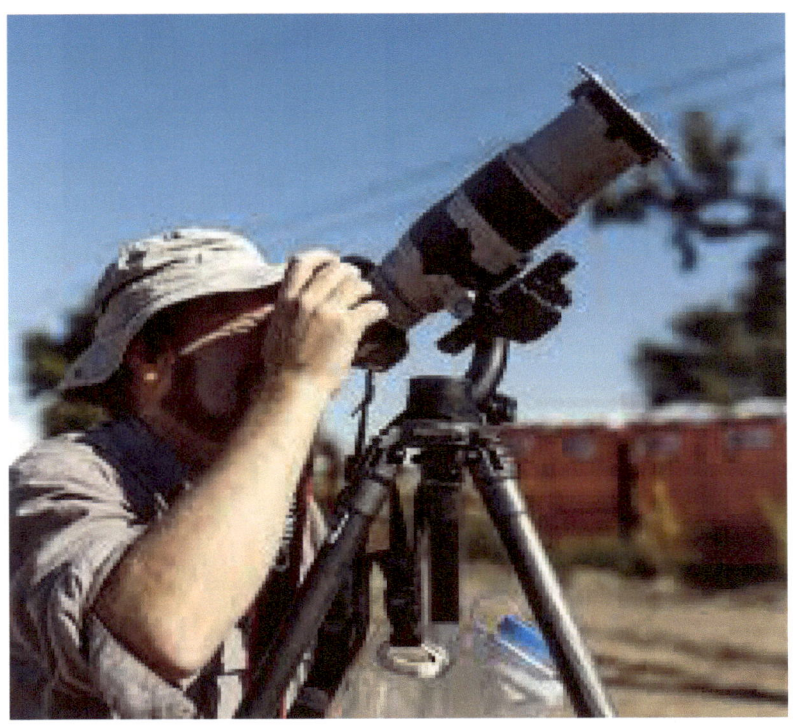

2. Plan Your Location: Scout for a location with a clear view of the sky, away from city lights and obstructions. Research the path of the eclipse or other phenomena to determine the best vantage point.

3. Practice Safety: Never look directly at the sun without proper solar filters, and ensure your camera lens has a solar filter or use a solar filter over the lens. This prevents damage to your eyes and equipment.

4. Use Manual Settings: Set your camera to manual mode to have full control over exposure, aperture, and ISO. For the eclipse, start with settings like ISO 100, f/8, and a shutter speed of 1/1000s, adjusting as needed based on lighting conditions.

5. Bracket Exposures: Capture multiple exposures of the same scene with different settings (underexposed, properly exposed, and overexposed). This helps in post-processing to achieve the best results.

6. Capture the Environment: Include elements like landscapes, people, or buildings in your shots to add context and scale to the astronomical event.

7. Experiment with Time-Lapse: Create stunning time-lapse videos of the eclipse or other phenomena by taking consecutive photos at regular intervals (e.g., every few seconds) and combining them in post-production.

8. Stay Patient and Observant: Astronomy photography requires patience and observation. Monitor the changing light conditions during the eclipse and adjust your settings accordingly to capture different phases effectively.

9. Post-Processing: Use software like Adobe Photoshop or Lightroom to enhance and edit your photos or videos, adjusting contrast, colors, and sharpness to bring out the details of the celestial event.

10. Share Your Work: Share your photographs or videos with astronomy communities, social media platforms, or submit them to astronomy publications to showcase your skills and contribute to the collective experience of celestial events.

Here are some fictional personal stories from individuals who have witnessed or participated in past eclipses, capturing their emotions and reflections:

Maria's Eclipse Expedition:

Maria, an avid astronomer, embarked on an expedition to witness the 2019 total solar eclipse in Chile. As the moon slowly covered the sun, Maria felt a rush of excitement and awe. She described the surreal experience of totality, with the sky darkening and stars becoming visible in the daytime. The moment the diamond ring effect appeared, Maria was overcome with emotion, feeling a deep connection to the universe and the wonders of nature. She returned from the expedition inspired, with a renewed passion for astronomy and a treasure trove of memories to cherish.

Tom's Eclipse Camping Trip:

Tom and his friends planned a camping trip to Oregon to view the 2017 total solar eclipse. As the eclipse approached, Tom couldn't contain his anticipation. When totality arrived, he was spellbound by the sight of the sun's corona shimmering in the darkened sky. Tom recalled feeling a sense of insignificance in the vastness of the cosmos, yet also a profound sense of unity with fellow eclipse watchers. The experience left Tom with a newfound appreciation for the beauty and harmony of celestial events.

Sarah's Eclipse Wedding:

Sarah and her partner decided to exchange vows during the 2020 annular solar eclipse. They chose a picturesque location with a clear view of the eclipse path. As the moon partially obscured the sun, casting a ring of fire in the sky, Sarah and her partner exchanged heartfelt promises. The symbolism of their love aligning with the celestial dance of the sun and moon was deeply meaningful to them. Sarah described the eclipse wedding as a magical and unforgettable moment that marked the beginning of their journey together.

David's Eclipse Outreach Event:

David, a science educator, organized a public outreach event for the 2018 partial solar eclipse. Families and enthusiasts gathered to observe the eclipse safely with solar viewers and telescopes. David was moved by the curiosity and wonder on people's faces as they witnessed a celestial event firsthand. Children asked questions about the science behind eclipses, and adults shared stories of past eclipse experiences. David felt gratified to inspire a love for astronomy in others and foster community engagement in science.

These personal stories capture the range of emotions and reflections experienced by individuals who have witnessed or participated in past eclipses, highlighting the transformative power and beauty of celestial phenomena.

General Questions

How long will the 2024 total solar eclipse last?
The longest duration of totality is 4 minutes, 28 seconds, near Torreón, Mexico. Most places along the centerline (path of totality) will see a totality duration between 3.5 and 4 minutes.

What does the path of totality mean?
The path of totality is where observers will see the Moon completely cover the Sun.

How much will daylight change during a total solar eclipse?
In the path of totality, where the Moon completely covers the Sun, the sky will become dark, as if it were dawn or dusk. For those who only experience a partial solar eclipse, the sky will appear slightly darker than it was before the eclipse, depending on how much the Moon blocks the Sun in their location.

How big of a temperature drop do you get during a total solar eclipse?
You can expect the temperature to drop about 10 degrees Fahrenheit (5 degrees Celsius) depending on the humidity and cloud cover at your location.

What are the stages of a total solar eclipse?
During a total solar eclipse, you will see multiple unique features as the eclipse progresses.

- Partial eclipse: As the Moon passes between the Sun and Earth, at first it does not completely cover the Sun. The Sun appears to have a crescent shape.
- Shadow bands: Shadow bands are rapidly moving, long, dark bands separated by white spaces that can be seen on the sides of buildings or the ground just before and after totality, though they can be very faint and difficult to photograph.
- Baily's Beads: As the Moon continues to move across the Sun, several points of light shine around the Moon's edges. Known as Baily's Beads, these are light rays from the Sun streaming through the valleys along the Moon's horizon
- Diamond Ring: Baily's Beads will begin to disappear until eventually, only a single bright spot will remain along the edge of the Moon's shadow. This bright spot resembles the diamond in a giant diamond ring formed by the rest of the Sun's atmosphere.
- Totality: Totality is when the Moon completely blocks the bright face of the Sun. This is the only stage of the eclipse that you can view with your naked eye. This stage can also reveal the chromosphere (a region of the solar atmosphere, appearing as the thin circle of pink around the Moon) and the corona

(the outer solar atmosphere, appearing as streams of white light).

After totality, viewers will be able to experience the features they saw earlier in the eclipse again.

Why is it not safe to look at the Sun even when only a small part of it is visible?

The rods and cones in the human retina are very sensitive to light. Normally during daylight conditions, the iris contracts so that only a small, safe amount of light passes through the lens and then reaches the retina. However, the Sun's surface is so bright that even a thin sliver of its light can still damage the eye if you were to look directly at it. When exposed to direct sunlight, retinal cells will become damaged, sometimes permanently. This can happen even after a quick glance at the Sun so it is very important to never look at the Sun directly. To look at the Sun, use solar viewing glasses or a property-equipped telescope.

Is it true that you should not look at the Sun even during a total solar eclipse?

When the bright photosphere of the Sun is completely covered, only the faint light from the corona is visible, and this radiation is too weak to have any harmful effects on the human retina. There is a misunderstanding that during a total solar eclipse, when the Moon has fully blocked the light from the Sun, there are still harmful rays that can injure your eyes. This is false.

During other types of solar eclipses, viewers must wear solar viewing or eclipse glasses or use an alternative viewing method the entire time, as at least part of the Sun is always visible. During a total solar eclipse, viewers should take those protective measures before and after the Sun's visible disk is completely blocked. However, once it's completely blocked – called totality – viewers can look directly at the eclipse without any special eye protection.

How are eyes damaged by staring at the Sun?
Typically, eye damage from staring at the Sun results in blurred vision, dark or yellow spots, pain in bright light, or loss of vision in the center of the eye (the fovea). Permanent damage to the retina has been shown to occur in ~100 seconds, but the

exact time before damage occurs will vary with the intensity of the Sun on a particular day and with how much the viewer's pupil is dilated from decongestants and other drugs they may be taking. Even when 99% of the Sun's surface (the photosphere) is obscured during the partial phases of a solar eclipse, the remaining crescent Sun is still intense enough to cause a retinal burn. Note, there are no pain receptors in the retina so your retina can be damaged even before you realize it, and by then it can be too late to save your vision!

Where can I get the right kind of solar filter to view the eclipse?
For a list of trusted solar filter vendors, please see the **American Astronomical Society's website**.

Is it only the bright light that is dangerous when viewing the Sun?
Although solar filters and eclipse glasses safely block the intense sunlight that is known to damage retinas, the infrared 'heat' from the Sun can also make viewing uncomfortable as it literally warms the eye. This is why staring at the Sun for minutes at a time even with proper filters can still overheat the tissues and fluids in the eye. The consequences of

this heating can be dangerous. To avoid this problem, frequently look away from the Sun to cool your eyes while using filters.

Can I photograph the eclipse with my smartphone?
Yes, but you need to have the specialized eclipse filter between your camera and the Sun.

How do modern-day scientists predict eclipses?
Astronomers first have to work out the geometry and mechanics of how Earth and the Moon orbit the Sun under the influences of the gravitational fields of these three bodies. From Newton's laws of motion, they mathematically work out the motions of these bodies in three-dimensional space, taking into account the fact that these bodies have finite size and are not perfect spheres. Scientists then feed the current positions and speeds of Earth and the Moon into these complex equations, and then program a computer to "integrate" these equations forward or backward in time to calculate the relative positions of the Moon and Sun as seen from the vantage point of Earth. Eclipses are specific configurations of these bodies that can be identified by the computer. Current eclipse forecasts are

accurate to less than a minute in time over a span of hundreds of years.

How rare are total solar eclipses?

During the 5,000-year period between 2000 BCE to 3000 CE, Earth will experience 11,898 eclipses of the Sun: 4,200 partial eclipses, 3,956 annular eclipses, 3,173 total eclipses and 569 hybrid eclipses. That means that every 1,000 years there are 840 partial eclipses, 791 annular eclipses, 635 total eclipses, and 114 hybrid eclipses. That works out to 2-3 solar eclipses of all kinds each year, and about 2 total solar eclipses every 3 years.

How is a total solar eclipse unique?

A total solar eclipse happens when the Moon passes between the Sun and Earth and completely blocks the face of the Sun. People located near the center of the Moon's shadow when it hits Earth will experience a total eclipse. The sky will become very dark, as if it were dawn or dusk. During a total solar eclipse, if skies are clear, people can see the Sun's outer atmosphere, the corona, with their own eyes. The corona is otherwise too dim to see against the bright face of the Sun. A total solar eclipse is the only type of solar eclipse where viewers can momentarily remove their eclipse glasses (not the same as ordinary sunglasses) for this brief period of time when the Moon is completely blocking the Sun. This is what will happen in the U.S. on April 8, 2024.

Why do NASA scientists' study solar eclipses?
NASA scientists study eclipses to make new discoveries about the Sun, Earth, and our space environment. Total solar eclipses are particularly important because they allow scientists to see a part of the Sun's atmosphere – known as the corona – that's too faint to see against the bright light of the solar disk.

How is the Sun completely blocked in a total eclipse?
Eclipses occur due to the special coincidence of the Moon and the Sun being the same angular size. The Sun is 400 times wider than the Moon, but it is also 400 times farther away, so they appear to be the same size in our sky. This is what allows the Moon to completely block the Sun during total solar eclipses.

EDUCATIONAL RESOURSES

Here's a list of recommended books, websites, and educational resources for readers interested in astronomy, eclipses, and related topics:

Books:

1. "Cosmos" by Carl Sagan - A classic exploration of the universe and our place in it.

2. "The Elegant Universe" by Brian Greene - Explores the fundamental nature of space, time, and the universe.

3. "Astronomy 101: From the Sun and Moon to Wormholes and Warp Drive, Key Theories, Discoveries, and Facts about the Universe" by Carolyn Collins Petersen - A comprehensive guide to astronomy basics.

4. "Eclipse: Journeys to the Dark Side of the Moon" by Frank Close - Explores the history and science of eclipses.

5. THE BEAUTY OF AURORA BOREALIS ; A Guide into the Mysteries of the Northern Lights by KATE OTTIS

Websites and Online Resources:

1. NASA's Eclipse Website - Offers information about upcoming eclipses, including detailed maps and viewing tips.

2. Sky & Telescope - A leading astronomy magazine with articles, guides, and resources for amateur astronomers.

3. Space.com - Covers space news, astronomy discoveries, and educational articles.

4. The European Southern Observatory (ESO) - Provides information about current astronomical research and discoveries.

5. The American Astronomical Society (AAS) - Offers resources for astronomers and the general public, including educational materials and event listings.

Educational Resources:

1. Coursera - Offers online courses in astronomy and related topics, often taught by leading experts in the field.

2. Khan Academy - Provides free courses and tutorials on astronomy, physics, and other sciences.

3. Stellarium - A free planetarium software that allows users to explore the night sky and learn about celestial objects.

4. The Astronomical Society of the Pacific - Offers educational materials, workshops, and resources for educators and the public.

5. YouTube Channels:

   - CrashCourse Astronomy

   - PBS Space Time

   - The Royal Observatory Greenwich

These resources cover a wide range of topics in astronomy, eclipses, and space exploration, suitable for both beginners and advanced enthusiasts.

www.ingramcontent.com/pod-product-compliance
Lightning Source LLC
Chambersburg PA
CBHW040323220526
45473CB00009B/2544